# EXPERIMENTS with FOOD

# Contents

1. What is Food? .................................................................... 5
2. Making Curd ..................................................................... 7
3. Water Solubility of Proteins .................................................. 8
4. Water ............................................................................... 9
5. Enzyme Activity ................................................................ 11
6. Diffusion .......................................................................... 13
7. Liquids ............................................................................ 15
8. Seed Germination ............................................................. 17
9. Surface Tension ................................................................ 19
10. Fermentation .................................................................. 21
11. Sugars ........................................................................... 22
12. Proteins ......................................................................... 23
13. Fats ............................................................................... 24
14. Respiration ..................................................................... 25
15. Beverage ........................................................................ 26
16. Testing Fruits .................................................................. 27
17. Testing Eggs ................................................................... 29
18. Chemical Reactions ......................................................... 30

# What is Food?

## Why do we eat food?

We eat food because it gives us energy. When foods are broken down in the body, energy is released. The larger the size of the body, the greater is the energy requirement.

## Do you know how food is formed?

We get food from both plant and animal sources. Green plants undergo the process of photosynthesis and manufacture food. They use carbon dioxide and water for the production of carbohydrates. Energy from the sun is utilised and oxygen is released. Some animals feed upon plants and obtain energy from them.

## Do you know what food is made up of?

Food is made up of proteins, fats, carbohydrates, vitamins and minerals. Water is also present in food. The water content of vegetables such as lettuce and cabbage and fruits such as watermelon is very high.

## Constituents of Food

**Carbohydrates** are made up of carbon, hydrogen and oxygen. These include sugars, starches and celluloses. Lactose in milk and glucose contain a lot of carbohydrates. These are present in cereals such as wheat, rice, maize, etc.

**Lipids** are greasy substances. They are also made up of hydrocarbons like the carbohydrates. They do not dissolve easily in water. These include vegetable oils and waxes, eg., groundnuts, mustard, coconut, etc.

**Proteins** are the most complex substances known. They are made up of carbon, hydrogen, oxygen and nitrogen. Many contain sulphur and phosphorus. Few proteins contain metallic elements such as iron, copper and zinc. Proteins are present in legumes such as lentils, beans and peas.

**Mineral** elements are required to maintain the growth and to repair the body tissues. Food should contain, in much smaller quantities, certain mineral elements. Bones require a lot of calcium phosphate. Sulphur occurs in combination with protein. Iron is an important part of haemoglobin and myoglobin. Zinc is required for insulin production. It is present in fruits like apple and banana.

**Vitamins** present in food are essential for maintaining health. These are organic substances required by the body in small amounts. They enable it to function properly. A deficiency of vitamins leads to certain diseases. Vitamins are present in oranges, mangoes and tomatoes.

Carbohydrates, proteins, lipids, minerals and vitamins should all be included in our daily diet. Everyone needs these nutrients, but the amounts needed vary from person to person.

# Making Curd

Certain small organisms exist which you cannot see with the naked eye. They are visible only under the microscope. These are called micro-organisms. Many of these organisms are of great economic value to man and on the other hand, many of them cause severe diseases.

## A useful effect of micro-organisms

**You will need:**
- a vessel
- milk
- one spoon of curd
- a spoon

1. Pour a glass of milk into a vessel.
2. Warm the milk slightly and add a spoon of curd to the milk.
3. Stir it slowly.
4. Cover the milk and leave it undisturbed for a few hours in a warm place. What do you observe?

The entire milk has solidified to form curd. When you added the spoonful of curd to the warm milk, bacteria present in it acted on the milk and solidified it to form curd. The quality of curd depends upon the quality of the milk and also upon the micro-organism used. *Lactobacillus* is used in the curdling of milk. During the formation of curd, casein protein of milk gets coagulated to form firm curd. Curd is good for health. It improves digestion and also increases appetite.

### Did you know?

Bacteria occur almost everywhere. They are found inside the human body, in soil, water and air. Nitrogen fixing bacteria are present in root nodules of leguminous plants and are very useful. There are others which cause deadly diseases. They are very minute. They can be rod shaped, spherical or spiral. They do not have a definite nucleus. When bacteria reproduce, each cell divides into two identical halves. Each half grows into a new one.

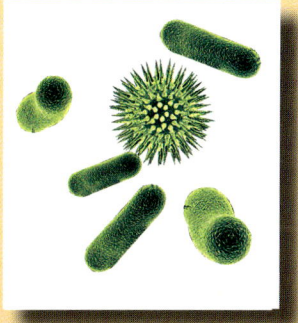

# Water Solubility of Proteins

Do you know that proteins are the most abundant molecules in cells? They form over half the dry weight of most organisms. They are also the instruments by which genetic information is expressed. In each cell of our body, there are thousands of different kinds of proteins.

Do you think that all proteins are equally soluble in water? Let us find out.

## Dissolving proteins in water

You will need:
- different proteins (albumin, casein)
- 2 test tubes
- water
- a stove

1. Take two different test tubes.
2. Half fill each with water.
3. Add a small quantity of the two different proteins to different test tubes. (Albumin is obtained from egg, and casein from milk.)
4. Shake the test tubes thoroughly.

## Do you see any foaming?

It means that the protein is soluble in water. If the protein is insoluble in cold water, you can try heating the water. Similarly, you can take different protein extracts and classify them as cold water soluble, hot water soluble and insoluble.

Different proteins have different functions. Haemoglobin is a protein present in blood which transports oxygen to different parts of our body. Seeds of many plants store nutrient proteins. These are required for the growth of the plant. Many proteins defend the body against invasion by other germs.

# Water

Water is the most abundant compound in living organisms. Do you know that the first living organisms probably existed in the oceans?

Water in food is very high. Turnip has ninety-three per cent water, potatoes have seventy-six per cent water, while green peas have seventy-eight per cent water. Water occurs in bound form also. Starch granules of rice bind water as cooking proceeds. Cellulose is present in food in the form of fibres in leaves and stems. It has a lot of water binding power.

## Detect the presence of water in food

**You will need:**
- Strips of cobalt chloride paper
- a hair-dryer
- food material such as pieces of sugarcane, boiled rice, boiled beans, boiled peas, pieces of coconut, slices of apple, mango and banana.

1. Take strips of cobalt chloride paper and dry them with a hair-dryer, till they are absolutely blue.

2. Fold them around the different food fragments.
3. Press them between dry glass slides.

## Do you observe any change in the colour of the cobalt chloride paper?

If there is moisture present in the food material, the paper will turn from blue to pink. This happens because cobalt chloride is blue when dry, and pink when in solution. The change from blue to pink is the test for water.

Water is a much better solvent than most common liquids. Sugars, alcohols, aldehydes and ketones readily dissolve in water. Substances dissolved in water, modify the particular properties of liquid water.

Water present in the food has a large number of functions in the human body. Water provides a transport medium for substances from one part of the body to another. Water is also the medium for the excretion of waste material. It enables the body to work at a near constant internal temperature.

# Enzyme Activity

Starch is a carbohydrate. It is made up of units of glucose. These are linked together to form a chain. It is relatively soluble in water. It is easily degraded into smaller fragments by the activity of enzymes. Two different kinds of starch molecules are found in plant cells. Starch is also a major food reserve in the seed.

## Degradation of starch by enzymes

**You will need:**
- rice
- water
- a stove
- a beaker
- test tubes
- a tile
- a dropper
- iodine solution

1. Wash the rice in a vessel, add water to it and put it on the stove for boiling.
2. Obtain 50 ml of the boiled rice water. Allow it to cool. This contains starch.
3. Obtain saliva from your mouth and transfer it to the beaker.
4. Dilute it by adding water.
5. Divide it into two parts in two different test tubes.
6. Boil the contents of one test tube.

7. Take two more tubes and label them as A and B.
8. In A put 2 ml of starch solution and 2 ml of fresh saliva solution.
9. In B put 2 ml of starch solution and 2 ml of boiled saliva solution.
10. Place both A and B test tubes in a beaker containing warm water.
11. Take a tile and with the help of a dropper, put drops of iodine solution on it.
12. At intervals of two minutes, take a drop of mixture from A and transfer it to one of the iodine spots.

# What do you see?

When the iodine solution comes in contact with the starch it turns blue-black. When the solution stops turning blue-black it means that all the starch has been digested.

Saliva contains the enzyme amylase. Amylase acts upon the starch and converts it into complex sugars. Initially, the amylase in the saliva is not able to convert all the starch into sugar. So it gives a positive test with iodine. As the time interval increases, all the starch present is converted into sugars by amylase. So iodine does not change the colour.

If you try the above test with the solution in test tube B, it will give a positive test for starch. Heat destroys the activity of the enzyme amylase.

Enzymes are proteins. They increase the rate of specific chemical reactions. They also require very mild conditions of temperature. The activity of enzymes can be altered by bringing changes in temperature or by adding heavy metals.

Do you know that rice starch has many uses? It has food value and is used in the laundry. It is used in the cosmetic industry and as a thickener in calico printing. It is utilised in the finishing of textiles and for making dextrins, glucose and adhesives.

# Diffusion

What happens when you put a vase of carnations in a room? The fragrance soon spreads in the entire room. What is this due to?

This is due to a process called diffusion. This is the process of the movement of molecules. When diffusion occurs, the molecules of one substance mix with the molecules of another substance. Molecules carrying the fragrance of the flowers, mix with molecules of air in the room. Diffusion can occur in solids, liquids and gases. When diffusion occurs the molecules move from a region where they are present in a large number to a region where they are present in a lesser number.

## Studying diffusion

**You will need:**
- a glass filled with water
- a few crystals of potassium permanganate

1. Put the crystals of potassium permanganate in the glass. What do you observe?

When you put the crystals of potassium permanganate in the water, the entire water becomes purple. This occurs because the crystals diffuse in the water. Potassium permanganate is used for disinfecting vegetables and fruits.

# Let us try another experiment

**You will need:**
- a pitcher
- a glass of water or milk
- one teaspoon of extract (such as peppermint, walnut, vanilla or almond)
- a glass
- a spoon

1. Pour the water or milk into the glass.
2. Add the extract and stir.

**You can drink it. Do you find it delicious?**
In the second experiment, a small amount of extract flavoured a large amount of water. The drink becomes delicious because the extract diffuses in the water. Extracts are made from the juices of meats, plants, herbs and flowers. Some extracts are made by squeezing the juices out of the original source. Other extracts are made by boiling the original source in water. Then the liquid is cooled and the water is removed by evaporation, leaving the extract.

# Liquids

Water is the most abundant substance in living systems. It makes up 70 per cent or more of the weight of most forms of life. Water has a higher melting point and boiling point than most common liquids. This shows that there are strong forces of attraction between the adjacent water molecules. What happens when you mix milk with water? The two mix so easily that it is difficult to distinguish one from the other. Let us see what happens when oil is mixed with water.

## Mixing oil and water

**You will need:**
- two small jars with lids
- red and blue food colouring
- water
- cooking oil
- a measuring cup
- 2 small containers

1. Write A on one jar and B on the second.
2. Take a small container and add a few drops of red food colouring to half a cup of water.
3. Similarly, pour half a cup of water into another small container. Add a few drops of blue food colouring to the water.
4. In jar A, pour one-fourth of the cup of red water, followed by one-fourth of the cup of blue water.
5. Cover the jar tightly and shake it vigorously. Set it down and observe it.

6. In jar B, pour one-fourth of the cup of red water.
7. Pour one-fourth of a cup of oil into this jar.
8. Cover the jar tightly and shake it vigorously.
9. Set the jar down and observe it.

## What happens?

You will see that in jar A, the red-coloured water and the blue-coloured water will mix completely to form a colour different from their original colours. In jar B, red water and oil do not mix completely with each other. They form separate layers. Two fluids which do not mix with each other are called immiscible. Oil and water are immiscible. Oils can be obtained from plant sources or animal sources. Soya bean, cottonseed, mustard, groundnut, sunflower and coconut are the plants which yield oil. Oily fish such as herring and pilchard are rich sources of marine oil.

# Exploring the Egg

Nutrients are required for the building up of the body. One of these is protein. Protein is present in both animal and plant food. Do you know the role of proteins? They provide material for the growth and repair of tissues. The nutritive value of a protein depends on the amino acid content. Animal proteins are present in milk, eggs, fish and meat. If these are not available, then adequate pulses can be taken.

## Studying egg proteins

**You will need:**
- 2 eggs
- oil
- a stove
- an iron plate
- plain paper
- coloured paper
- scissors

1. Crack the egg and separate the white from the yolk. Take the help of an adult.
2. Now trace out the shape of a bird on the coloured paper.
3. With the help of scissors cut along the lines to get the shape of a bird.
4. Apply egg white behind the coloured paper.
5. Now try to stick it on the plain sheet of paper.

17

# Let us try another experiment

1. In the presence of a trusted adult, put the iron plate on the stove.
2. Pour one to two spoons of oil on the plate.
3. Now sprinkle some salt over it and crack an egg.
4. After the egg is cooked remove it from the plate.

Do you know that egg whites were used to attach gold leaf to early, hand-written books? The golden decorations added beauty to the books.

When a solution of a protein, like the egg albumin, is slowly heated to about 60 or 70°C, the solution gradually becomes cloudy and a coagulum is formed. The white of the egg contains the albumin. It coagulates to a white solid on heating. If you try to cool the solution, the egg white will not redissolve to give a clear solution.

# Surface Tension

Do you know why drops of rain become spherical? This is due to the property of liquids called surface tension. There is a tension in the free surface of the liquid which acts equally in all directions and at all points in the surface.

Surface tension has many practical uses. One is in the cleaning of dirty clothes. When the detergent or soap solution is added to water, the surface tension between the water and the grease in the clothes is reduced. So it carries away the greasy dirt with it.

## Another example of surface tension

**You will need:**
- capillary tubes made of glass
- a glass filled with water

1. Dip the capillary tubes inside the glass filled with water.

**What do you see?**

The water level rises in the tubes. This is an effect of the surface tension of water.

## Creating surface tension

**You will need:**
- half a cup of milk
- food colouring (four colours)
- two steel plates
- liquid detergent
- half a cup of water

1. Pour the milk into the plates.
2. Carefully place about the drops of each food colouring on the milk.
3. Add three or four drops of soap near the side of the plate.
4. Continue to add soap.

## What happens?

The drops of food colour slowly spread on the surface of milk assuming a spherical shape. These then join together to form a thin film. When the soap solution is poured dropwise, it spreads to form a film. This film cuts into the film formed by the joining of the food colours. So the soap solution changes the surface tension between the milk and the food colouring.

When water is used instead of milk, the food colours penetrate the water surface and diffuse deep inside the water. They do not form a film.

# Fermentation

It is the process by which glucose is degraded into various products for obtaining energy. Yeast and other micro-organisms ferment the glucose into ethanol and carbon dioxide. In 1856, Louis Pasteur showed that micro-organisms cause the fermentation of sugar to yield alcohol. Do you know that yeasts are abundantly present in material which contain sugars? They can also be found in milk, in plants and in the soil!

## Yeast activity

**You will need:**
- a plate
- wheat flour
- water
- sugar
- yeast powder and milk

1. Warm the water on the stove.
2. Add a little sugar and a tablespoon of milk to it.
3. Put a handful of flour on the plate. Add two spoons of yeast to it.
4. Slowly pour the sweet water in the flour and knead it so that it assumes a spherical shape.
5. Keep the dough under your constant observation.

### What do you see?

You will find that the size of the dough increases considerably. It starts rising. Holes appear in the dough.
How can you explain it? The holes appear in the dough when the yeast starts acting on the sugar present in it and carbon dioxide is released. It is due to this that the dough enlarges and becomes puffy. This is fermentation.

# Sugars

Have you tried chewing sugarcane during the winters? It is delicious, and chewing it is a good exercise for the teeth. The sugar crystals which we eat are obtained from this cane. Sugar gives us energy and makes our food sweet. All green plants make food in the form of sugar. Let us make a drink, with and without sugar, and see the difference between the two.

**You will need:**
- 2 glasses
- water
- a lemon
- salt
- sugar
- a knife

1. Pour water in the two glasses.
2. Now cut a lemon into two.
3. In one glass, mix two spoons of sugar.
4. In the other glass mix some salt.
5. Now squeeze the lemon into both the glasses.
6. Stir properly with a spoon.

## Do you find any difference in the taste of the two preparations?

Which one tastes better? Adding sugar to a drink makes a world of difference.

Do you know that sugar is used to preserve things? It is used in fruits, jams and jellies. It is also used in the making of soft drinks and ice-creams.

Before sugar began to be made, honey was used as a sweetening agent. Honey is the nectar collected from flowering plants by bees. It is a source of sugars, proteins, minerals and water. It is also used in medicines.

# Proteins

Do you know that proteins form one of the most important components of our diet? These proteins are also found in the cells of living organisms. A single cell can contain hundreds of different kinds of proteins.

## Does wheat contain protein?

**You will need:**
- a small plastic tub
- wheat flour
- a glass full of water
- a few grains of pulses
- coloured thread
- a piece of cardboard

1. Put the wheat flour in a plastic tub.
2. Add some water to the wheat flour.
3. Now mix the flour thoroughly with the water, till the paste turns into a hard mass.
4. Make two spherical pieces of dough.
5. Put them on the cardboard so that they stick to each other.
6. Press some grains of pulses together so that they form the eyes and nose of a eat (see figure).
7. Use the strands of thread to form the cat's whiskers.

## Why did the wheat flour stick together?

This is due to a protein called glutenin found in wheat. It gives elasticity to the dough made from wheat flour.

There is a protein present in egg white called ovalbumin. Casein is a protein present in milk.

# Fats

Do you like having peanut-butter sandwiches? They are a good source of energy as they contain fats. Fats are also present in meat and eggs. Natural fats are present in olive oil. Linseed oil is a plant oil used as a base for paints. It is very rich in fatty acids.

## Peanut butter

**You will need:**
- 250 grams of peanuts
- a cup of milk
- bread
- a bowl
- a grinder
- paper

1. Ask a trusted adult to set the grinder for you.
2. Put the peanuts inside the grinder and switch it on.
3. Transfer the powdered peanuts to a bowl.
4. Now slowly add some milk till a paste is formed.
5. Apply the peanut butter on a slice of bread and enjoy it.

Take a few peanuts, crush them and rub them on paper.
Do you see the stain on the paper? This stain is due to the oil present in the peanuts. Fats are greasy in nature and insoluble in water.

Fats are made up of fatty acids. Sometimes these acids form waxes. There are glands present in the skin which secrete waxes. Waxes not only give protection to the skin of animals but also keep it waterproof. Hair, wool and fur are coated with waxy secretions. Waxes are not only present in animals, but also in plants. They give a shiny appearance to the leaves of many plants.

# Respiration

Have you tried to breathe out in the open on a cold day? You must have seen tiny droplets of water vapour in your breath. Similarly, plants also try to breathe out through their leaves. An exchange of gases takes place between the leaves and the external atmosphere. Plants take in carbon dioxide and give out oxygen. So they purify the air.

## How do plants breathe?

**You will need:**
- a healthy potted plant with many green leaves
- a plastic bag
- string

1. Water the potted plant properly. Let the excess water drain out through the hole in the base.
2. Put a plastic bag over the plant. Use a string to tie the bag around the small pot.
3. Place the pot near a sunny window.
4. Observe the plant the next day.

### What do you see?

There are droplets of water present on the inside of the bag. This water is given out by the leaves of the plant during transpiration. Loss of water vapour in transpiration occurs through the stomata in the epidermis. Stomata are present not only in the leaves but also in certain fruits like banana. Plants that grow in dry environments and in areas which receive a lot of light have small and more numerous stomata than those in wet and shaded environments. Many broad-leaved plants have stomata on both the surfaces of the leaf. Most of the water absorbed by the roots is lost by transpiration.

# Beverage

What do you do if you feel very tired? Most probably you will either take a glass of milk or a cup of tea. Tea leaf extract has stimulatory properties. Do you know that the tea we drink actually comes from the leaves of the tea plant? The leaves of the tea plant have a typical fragrance.

## Make a cup of tea

**You will need:**
- milk (one-third of a glass)
- water (two-thirds of a glass)
- tea leaves (one teaspoon)
- sugar (two teaspoons)
- a vessel
- a stove

1. Add some milk to the water and pour it in the vessel.
2. Put the vessel on the stove.
3. Add the sugar and tea leaves.
4. Let it boil.
5. Turn off the stove and pour the tea in a glass through a strainer.

There are many kinds of tea, namely black tea, green tea, oolong tea and brick tea. Tea leaves contain amino acids, sugars and organic acids. There is an oil called theol present in tea leaves. This gives the flavour to tea. A cup of tea provides a lot of calories. It also contains B complex vitamins.

# Testing Fruits

The pistil of a flower changes to form the fruit. Fruits can be dry or succulent. Succulent fruits contain sugar. When they have flavour and aroma, they are both attractive and edible. Fruit contains the reserve food material from the main plant.

Have you observed a bruised fruit?

A bruised fruit is damaged and becomes brown. Certain compounds called phenols are present in fruits. These get converted to quinones which form dark brown pigments.

## Enzymic browning in fruits

**You will need:**
- fruits (apple, banana, pear, grape)
- a knife

1. Cut thin slices from each fruit.
2. Leave the slices exposed for about thirty minutes.

Do you see the browning of the slices? Record the degree of browning. Let us now study the conditions which affect browning.

1. Cut similar segments from one fruit.
2. Leave one segment intact.
3. Dice the second segment.
4. Cut the third segment into four fragments.
5. Bruise the fourth segment slightly.
6. Leave the fifth segment in a warm room.
7. Leave the sixth segment in the refrigerator.

**Do you see any difference in browning under different conditions?**

Prevent the browning of fruits
1. Take a fruit and cut similar segments.
2. Leave one segment immersed in water.
3. Immerse the second segment in water for thirty seconds, then leave it exposed.
4. Immerse the third segment in vinegar solution for thirty seconds, then leave it exposed.
5. Immerse the fourth segment in boiling water for thirty seconds, then leave it exposed.
6. Leave the fifth segment exposed without any treatment.
7. Compare the results.

Did you obtain any success in preventing the browning of fruits?

Fruits are rich in minerals and vitamins. Besides, they contain dissolved sugars and pectins.

# Testing Eggs

An egg is a living organism consisting of an embryo and is a storehouse of food enclosed in a shell. The shell consists chiefly of chalk (calcium carbonate) with small quantities of calcium phosphate and organic matter. The egg yolk is a golden yellow fluid mass enclosed in a thin elastic membrane. The white of an egg or the egg albumen is protein in nature. 70 % of the egg white protein is ovalbumin.

## Foaming properties of egg white

**You will need:**
- test tubes
- egg white
- water
- detergent

1. In one test tube place 2 cm level water and 2 cm level egg white.
2. Place 4 cm level water and a few drops of washing detergent in another test tube.
3. Shake both the test tubes and compare the foam produced.
4. Allow both the test tubes to stand, and compare their stability.

## Is the egg fresh?

**You will need:**
- salt
- water
- a vessel
- a tall jar
- 2 eggs (fresh and old)

1. Dissolve 10 gm salt in one litre water. Pour it in a tall jar.
2. Place the egg in the tall jar.
3. Repeat this with the other egg. What do you observe?

   This test is called the Brine test. The fresh egg will sink in the solution and lie flat at the bottom of the jar. The older egg will float in the solution. The older egg has lost weight due to the evaporation of water. Shrinkage and drying of the contents enlarges the air chamber. So the egg becomes more buoyant.

# Chemical Reactions

Carbon dioxide is a normal constituent of the atmosphere. It is a harmless, colourless gas, almost odourless and tasteless. Do you know that carbon dioxide can be produced by chemical reaction?

All carbonates react with acids. An acid reacts with carbonate to produce salt and water and carbon dioxide.

## Produce carbon dioxide

**You will need:**
- a vinegar sample
- a fruit juice sample
- a sour milk smaple
- pH papers
- test tubes

1. Use pH papers to find out the pH of vinegar, fruit juice and sour milk by dipping the papers into these liquids.
2. Now pour sodium bicarbonate in three test tubes.
3. Add vinegar, fruit juice and sour milk to the above test tubes, respectively. What do you observe?

Can you see the production of carbon dioxide gas in the test tube? If you want to test the nature of the gas, pass it through lime water. It will turn milky.

Do you know that the simplest artificial vinegar consists of industrial acetic acid well diluted with water and coloured with a little caramel? Such vinegar has harshness and pungency.